MOTHER, NATURE

Aoife Lyall (*née* Griffin) was born in Dublin in 1987. She earned her BA in English Studies from Trinity College Dublin, before reading her MPhil in Medieval Literature at St John's, University of Cambridge, and gaining her PGDE (English) at the University of Aberdeen.

Awarded an Emerging Scottish Writer residency by Cove Park in 2020 and twice shortlisted for the Hennessy New Irish Writing Awards, her poems have also been shortlisted in the Wells Festival of Literature Open Poetry Competition and the Jane Martin Poetry Prize. She was longlisted for the inaugural Rebecca Swift Foundation Women Poets' Prize in 2018. Her first collection, *Mother, Nature*, was published by Bloodaxe Books in 2021.

She has worked as a guest curator for the Scottish Poetry Library and as a guest editor for *Butcher's Dog*. Her reviews have appeared in *Browse*, *The Interpreters' House*, *PN Review* and *Poetry London*.

She lives and works in the Scottish Highlands with her family.

AOIFE LYALL

Mother, Nature

BLODAXE BOOKS

ISBN: 978 1 78037 518 2

First published 2021 by
Bloodaxe Books Ltd,
Eastburn,
South Park,
Hexham,
Northumberland NE46 1BS.

www.bloodaxebooks.com
For further information about Bloodaxe titles
please visit our website and join our mailing list
or write to the above address for a catalogue

Supported using public funding by
**ARTS COUNCIL
ENGLAND**

Cover design: Neil Astley & Pamela Robertson-Pearce.

Printed in Great Britain by Bell & Bain Limited, Glasgow, Scotland, on
acid-free paper sourced from mills with FSC chain of custody certification.

To my children –

Here, I hold you all.

CONTENTS

PREFATORY NOTE

I had little exposure to the reality of pregnancy or early motherhood until I became pregnant in 2015. Having excelled at Biology in school, I was shocked by how ignorant I was, and how systemically I was kept in the dark as my pregnancy progressed: I learned about conception in class, but no one taught me about let-down, uterine cramps or postnatal bleeding until I was in my third trimester; I understood how my body would support the baby, but not how it would be irreparably changed and damaged in the process; I knew how to draw the male and female reproductive systems, but didn't see a diagram of a breast until my youngest was four months old. I was told of the importance of breast feeding, but not how much it hurts. Or about mastitis or tongue-tie, cluster feeds or 'wonder' weeks. In short, I knew how to beget a child: not how to become a mother.

That said, nothing prepares you for the loss of a child. I turned to what I knew and found only more absence, more silence: I could recall no poem or story to lean into or rail against; no song or film to interrogate or take comfort in. Surrounded by the loss of life, the loss of potential life is deemed unrecognisable, almost unconscionable: something for which grief is indulgent, mourning indecent. And so the years gain a calendar of quiet anniversaries. The positive pregnancy test and the first doctors' appointment. Perhaps the first scan; perhaps the second. Then the day something doesn't feel right. The trip to the hospital. Finally, the due date, never now a birthday. And through it all, the silence. Such silence.

It's not just loss: it's a loss of confidence. I was disabused of the myth that my maternal will could safeguard my children; shown that the world could get through my deepest, most intimate defences. It took a long time for conviction to overcome doubt, for pragmatism to gain a foothold over fear, for purpose to return to function, for joy to return to purpose. And then your time is up. You find a childminder. Go back to work. Divide yourself into smaller and smaller pieces to be gathered up and put back together, but never again capturing the entire picture.

Raised in anti-abortion Ireland, I was constantly surrounded by maternal morality essays, movies about the Magdalene laundries, and lengthy debates about the legitimacy of dehumanising human rights. And yet, the deep and profound injustice of the State's position still didn't fully register until, just weeks pregnant, I read an article about an Irish couple in the UK who had, and made, the choice to terminate an unviable pregnancy: a decision that, at the time, would have earned them a prison sentence and criminal record in Ireland. For the first time I was afraid of what it meant to be Irish: afraid of what my own country could force me to endure; afraid for the friends and family who could find themselves in, or on, the same boat. My poem 'Acrania' came from a need to confront and expose a complex emotional conflict at play. And, for a long time, it was the first poem in the manuscript, followed by a sequence that endeavoured to capture the joy in grief, and the grief in joy, now so familiar to me. It was only as the manuscript reached its final stages that was I able to move 'Acrania' to the back and allow my own experience of loss to come forward and speak for itself.

To say a piece of work is classic or timeless, that it has risen above and been experienced beyond its context, is to give it a great compliment. I didn't want that for 'Acrania'. I wanted to keep that poem, that experience, on its very Irish streets. To return to the poem after the abortion referendum in 2018 and mark it *out-of-date*, was a significant moment for me: it spoke to a fundamental purpose of poetry; to observe, to record, and to give voice to the present before it becomes an inevitable, and untouchable, past.

Sounds of that day

(after Norman MacCaig)

When a silence came,
it was your heart not beating.
When the door hushed, it was
the shuffle of a midwife leaving
us alone in our private grief. A muffled clanging
ten yards down the corridor was the news breaking and
unbreaking in the filing cabinet.
When the black biro rolled, it was me
falling and falling into myself.

When the door
clicked shut behind us, it was the end
of all the silences there were.

They left us
in the busiest corridor in the hospital.

I thought I was hurt in my body only
not knowing that
when your body sleeps
your mind feels all those kicks
in your round stomach before you wake
and the whole world goes numb.

Ubi Sunt

Where are the sleepsuits, the scratch mitts, the car seat?
Where are the bassinet, the basket, and the bag?
Where are the bath, the playmat, and the pillow?

Is this the right corridor? Is this the right room?

Where are the smiling faces and the nodding heads?
Where are the screenshots and the photographs?
Where are your heartbeats and your small breaths?

Is this all there is? Is this all I get?

Where are the smiles, the cards, and well-wishes?
Where are the midnight feeds and midday naps?
Where are the songs? Where are the words?

Hospital Canteen

It may be possible
to give you a scan picture.
Please bring exact money.
Change cannot be given.

Its shiny flat surface looks so fragile
in the cashier's hands I have to stop
myself from telling her to hold it
      by the edges
from pointing out all the newness
how the otters' backs curve
how their soft faces turn
how their legs rest fluent
and frozen in time like
the baby I never saw
on the screen as blank
as the black coffee
I queue to cradle
in my hands
the change a secret
a cenotaph I leave
for someone else to find.

The grave diggers

Worn smooth, their shovels, picks, and sombre
mattocks congregate by the tarpaulin shroud.

It is slow work. They must be thorough:
there must be width and breadth and scope

for more. Normally a chatty bunch, they give
the smallest graves their silence, their job

to turn this hallowed hollowed ground of mine
from grave to garden with the little dignity

such deconsecration can afford. A labour
of love, they pause to pay their last respects,

leave me with my immeasurable silence,
expecting nothing in return.

No flowers: by request

And still they come. The lilies burst
like corpses, waft their death scent
through the open house. A wake

for weeks I am the grave they send
the lilies to. Exhumed and made ready
my body rich with loam I watch them

wither until they rot and stain my clothes
until with my own hands I have to leave
them in the garden to sink into the soil

the coffin-brown lid of the compost bin
nailed shut by midwives' hands, florists'
smiles, black biros waiting for a signature.

Haunted

Baby books lie buried   beneath the spare bed
moved there weeks ago   by well-intentioned mothers while
winter onesies obscured   in the nursery wardrobe
tumble into my lap   price-tags blood-red and sharp while
leaflets and pamphlets lie concealed   among the circulars
to tell their untold stories   under the stairs while
paper apparitions   slip through the letterbox
appointment reminders   ripped up and recycled while
phonecalls rebound   with the repeated question
Guess who's pregnant now?   and I am made to guess
hidden by the empty home   my body has become

Month's Mind

We don't know which ones we're meant to bring
so we settle on the yellows for all the sorrys
there are. We pick the smallest bunch. Full
of buds, but no flowers, we lay them to rest
in the river. Our slow footsteps mourn the dying
shadows as we walk back to the house together

and alone. Once home, we bury our good shoes
at the bottom of the wardrobe. We pour the tea
and unwrap plates of sandwiches and cake.
In low voices we talk a little about the life
you never lived, and the house you never lived in
is overwhelmed by all the people who didn't know to come.

Octopus

They crochet them for premature babies:
it stops the lonely reach and tug of the thin
plastic lifelines on the neonatal wards.
They find instead the thick pulsing twist
of an umbilical octopus, and wrap their fists
around its tentacles, calmed by the curling
thoughts of their absent mothers.

So I tell the man behind the till it's for you
this plush octopus all tentacles and soft stitching.
Home, price pulled off and care label cut,
I rest him on the marbled coral of my stomach.
I watch him float on the tide of rising limbs
that twist and curl beneath him, my octopus,
my omphalos buoyed by the living current.

Silent Movie

The camera work is imperfect.
Unsure at times, you pause mid-
motion, stuck in absurd

positions and poses, or else
seem to miss a beat and
skip ahead in a series of mismatched

edits. The only sound is a chorus
of whispers from your captive audience
unable to picture you in colour, still.

And all too soon the performance ends
and I am left to stare at the blank
screen of my projected stomach.

I stay this way long after your one-man
show has ended, always waiting
for that little something after the credits.

Your name

Sea glass on other tongues
I polish the rough-cut syllables
to radiant sapphires. I bury them
in a chest of blood and bone.

Lips sealed in the harsh island light
your name is the folded treasure map
I hide in my throat: when I am lost
it will lead me back to you. Marked

with the dangers such knowledge
brings, my skin stretches and stretches:
longitudes and latitudes etched
into a world that will never be flat again.

Starry Night

A canvas of bubbles stretches
across the surface of the water.
Jewelled with the yellow globules
of insoluble stars, filigreed with indigo
swirls, the clouded sky is broken only
by the dome of my stomach. Your small
kicks ripple the static scene, and the village
pulses once more with the life and death,
starts and stops, of the intangible artist.

Hermit Crab

I am your home
Hold me close and you can hear the ocean

Soon you will outgrow me
And gravitate to greater echoes

Moses basket, cot, bed
Shadowed by parents who marvel at your fragility

In each new space
You grow and grow into, grow and grow out of

The room, the house
The street too small for your itchy feet

You will cast your net wide
As you grow into the world (careful pet, not to burn your fragile skin)

I will wait here
Shell of a home (I hope you find a shell that fits us both)

Until at last
After a day at the beach

You line me up on the mantelpiece
With conches, driftwood, heart-shaped rocks

And marvel at how we grow
And shrink into the worlds around us

Vaudeville

STRONGMAN: You muscle into the space around you
lie on your back to juggle and pummel
the ceiling of your convex stage with new
found feet and new formed fists

ACROBAT: In love with how your body moves
enthralled by its joyful back flips
and flip-flops, your long limbs
whirl and unfurl in the heady melee

COMEDIAN: You flail about in outrageous ways
impossible protrusions and sudden dips
propel you straight-faced and inscrutable
across your spot-lit stage

DANCER: You slow things down with a gentle
routine of elbows and knees and
hands and feet wrapped around
the vaulted ribs of your private theatre

MAGICIAN: You astound and amaze with a flurry
of quick tricks and slapstick and leave
your audience completely unaware
of how you can, and do, disappear in there

Easter Sunday

I do not know the hour of your arrival
so I mark them all, sanctifying the night

with offerings of soft light and snatches
of old songs. Devoted to you, the clicks

of my hips tell half-remembered rituals
and prayers. With bended knees I wait

for the tell-tale streaks of light to stretch
across the ceiling. Then I will roll the stone

of my stomach back from the bed, and wonder
when I will believe that I have risen with new life.

Epithalamion

I carry you to our first bed, honoured
by guarded women who avert
their wisdom and whisper *You soon
forget the pain. It's worth it.*

In the end. I lie back and think of you.
An expectant hush turns all heads towards
the cotton veil and there you are. Dressed
in your finest vernix, you only have eyes for me.

You have my eyes, my hands, my hair.
You are the declaration of love.
You are the dowry, the wedding gift,
the vows, the midnight dancing.

Labour

Pitched headfirst into a sea
of blood and broken waters
all I know is a sodden bed
and a plastic tube
between my teeth.

Contractions crash through me.
I beg   I bargain   I promise
Screams splinter in my mouth. Sweat
slicks the sheets they can't change fast
enough. My hamstring cramps.
My pelvis pulls itself apart. Oblique
muscles tear like cotton
with every encouraging cry of
push   *push*   *push*
my skin rips with every
just   *one*   *more*
and there you are.

Skin and muscle, cry and mouth.
When they cut the cord my heart
breaks and I cry like a mother
desperate for her baby.

After birth

The room is awash with paediatricians
and surgeons. They cut and stitch like fishermen,
gut and clean like fishermen's wives. Your father
plucks you from their blue-green sea, your skin
still salmon-pink from the struggle, and when
he kisses you for the first time all at once, his eyes
fill with the knowledge of the whole world in his hands.

Epidural

(after Emily Dickinson)

After great pain, a formal feeling comes —
the nerves calmed and tempered and put to sleep —
and my exhausted heart worries *Will I know him*
when I see him? Will I know that he is mine?

The monitors, mechanical, beep
and sound in their impersonal way —
I drift between the ground and air —
with only a numb content to hold me

to the moment. This, then, is the final hour —
the one to be remembered and outlived —
as other mothers whispered once before
first the pain — the push — the letting go.

Treasure island

Unadorned but for the clip
on your umbilical cord, we are
skin to skin.

The blue paper curtain
oceans our island. It is full of treasure.

Here is my mother's necklace, unclasped
and heirloomed in cotton wool.

Here, the watch my father gave me:
how easily time slides and twists
over a naked wrist.

Here, my wedding-rings take the light
and with it their pledge and promise.
I lay them aside and lift you

to my chest, my treasure. There,
you unlock my motherself
and find it full of riches.

Syzygy

You sleep on my chest
        hands splayed like a sunset
   on muslin clouds after a
storm of tears, the moon
    of your mouth pulling
      the tide of my milk
        the sound of the ocean
          in every breath.

Caledonian sleeper

Nothing more than a berth between us
the hours pass like midnight carriages.

We journey through them like villages
hamlets of half-formed thoughts and dreams.

Your soft snores signal our Highland route
your restless stops and starts disturb the rhythm

of the sleepers. Unaccustomed to your silences
we lie and listen to you sleep, eyes full

of the darkness between each starry breath.

Ships in the night

I lift you like a lax sail catching the wind.
Eyes sealed against the rose-tinted light
your father carries you to the changing table

careens your keening body with quiet love,
keeps me steady as I moor you to my breast
and you take your fill of its milk-warm lullaby.

Semaphored to bed, his stern shoulders
slip through our soft shadows. Set down
in still waters, the tug of sleep –

Minute and far away

Through the heavy fog of broken sleep, I see them.
Reflected in the kitchen cupboard, their green light

appears and disappears across the room. Always
on standby, theirs is a silent siren song. I sense

it all: the cup, the capsule, the coffee, the milk
frothed and spooned on top with just a touch

of cinnamon. I live in the potential of that first sip
for hours while you sleep on me, stopped only

by the knowledge that the push and puncture
will wake the house and leave us all diminished.

Soft spot

I watch your father's daily habit.
Smart trousers, pressed shirt
shirtsleeves carefully rolled back,

he peels potatoes at the kitchen sink, guiding
the knife under the soil-soaked potato
skin as gentle as the first time

he held you sleeping, thumbing the smell
from your newborn head, easing around
the knots, the soft spot, humming.

Fully Comp

Running late, the midwife asks you to wait
the time it takes to get into her gloves but you
are eight days overdue and ready to be born
your head a world of continental plates
hurtling through this finite, bounded space
where instinct drives me and I push you
through the viscous sting of separating
skin so eight days later, when your father
hears the car doors shriek tectonic against
the unforgiving pillar and doesn't think
to stop, reverse and angle for more room,
I understand the need to put the foot down
and push against the odds, only to marvel
at the damage and wonder at the cost.

Silt

It gathers in the riverbeds and basins of your hands.
You hold it tight in your small fists: it is the tenuous
grasp you have on the world and you resist when I
try to loosen it. Asleep, I unfurl each newborn finger
and, with the tip of my smallest nail, lift the daily
sediment away. Beneath, the long lines of your life,
your head, your heart, run still and deep: your future
mapped out in miniature, tucked into the steadfast
folds and creases of your palms.

Saturn

Surrounded by the dirt and detritus of half-
eaten meals and half-finished lists
you feed and sleep and feed and sleep.

The day wears on. The circumference
spreads. The dust gathers. The dishes swirl.
A fly satellites: it threatens and threatens

to land. Curled into my stomach, you cut
a path through the debris of cluster feeds
and make it beautiful. You wake and cry.

The sound rings out from our quiet
corner of the universe. Your tears fall
like diamonds: my milk flows like rain.

equilibrium (noun)

1. *Chemistry* A state in which a process and its reverse are occurring at equal rates so that no overall change is taking place.

> *We are water. Broken, unbroken*
> *we are ice, and sea, and sky.*
> *Love does not alter.*

2. *Economics* A situation in which supply and demand are matched.

> *Flood me with oxytocin.*
> *Fill these veins with liquid gold.*
> *Hush, darling. This mine*
> *will never empty.*

3. A state in which opposing forces or influences are balanced.

> *We will rise and crash*
> *upon each other*
> *at the changing*
> *of the tide.*
> *Dredging petty rips*
> *and trenches, we will carve*
> *the shapes of traps and expectations.**

* But we are water. Broken, unbroken, we are ice, and sea, and sky. And love does not alter.

Aqua vitae

I know when you've had enough. Sprawled
across my lap, I heave you to your feet
and lay you on my chest to sleep it off.

One unfocused eye furrows open and stares
in my direction before your hands stretch
and your head falls and you sigh and sleep

one hand nestled in my armpit, the other lying
prostrate by your side. And always your left ear
pressed against my heart. This heart. Here.

*　*　*

Origami
from a single cell
folded
and unfolded
you are art and science
the maths
cannot explain
you   you cannot exist
without it
minute by hour
day by week
your folds unfurl
lily
swan
fortune teller
leaping frog
the folds in
your ears
a secret
passed down
through
your father's
father's
father's

Sacrum

Your back arches at the touch of gel as smooth
on your skin as the vernix it barely remembers.
The radiographer works in silence, curving
the transducer with the rhythm of a song, playing
the scales of your spine with her crystal probe.
On screen, your tiny vertebrae undulate into seas
that boil and rage, subside and rise again as Alps,
Cairngorms, and Macgillycuddy's Reeks, only
to collapse into dunes and dust, and be swept back
into the sea in this side room where you have fallen
asleep to the finities and infinities inside you.

Conditions of Sale

Only if cancelled due to miscarriage
or similar circumstances
will you receive a full refund.

I lay you down in your new cot.
Twelve weeks old, you stretch your limbs
into the oblivion of space and sleep.

Downstairs, your father swaddles
the Moses basket in plastic sheets.
Careful not to tear them, he tucks
the price tags in.

Autumn

You sleep as your father changes sheets,
switches quilts, airs blankets for an early
winter. As he wraps and vacuum-packs
our long summer in the spare room

my pen scatters letters like leaves on the page
patterns them into words like *grief* and *loss*
and *longing* to make this poem a living thing
when it is rooted in absence and empty soil.

Next door, the neighbours' husky howls,
lamenting the people who have left him.
Listless I listen, longing for the intensity
of his grief, the impermanence of his loss.

Trapeze

My life revolves around you. I must
learn the art of balances, hangs and
drops as you look to me for life.

The lack of sleep. The near misses.
The aching doubts. I practise *natural*
until I cannot see myself.

There is no room for error.
Toes curled, cast out, I freefall
through the week. If I open

my eyes to the chance of falling,
I will fall. And down will come baby,
cradle and all.

3oz

The rhythm of your silence is ours, the one we
learned together in the long nights of early days
when, eyes shut, you wrapped one hand around
my little finger and, with the other, held my hand
as I tried not to cry. I felt your stomach fill
with the violent sting of golden milk.
My body bled for you. My collarbone cradled the soothers
that slipped from your sleeping lips
as I carried you to bed. Settled, I slipped between
the milk-stained sheets and slept until you needed me again.

Now content in your father's arms, you swallow
thin grey formula from a lukewarm plastic bottle.
I leave the room and pretend to do the dishes.
The water is cold and fills an empty sink.

Seabed

When you fuss, your father turns
from cliff face to cove and curls
you into him, his steady breath
the swell that brings you home.

Ithaca

I felt the empty vibrations
for weeks my fingers hunted
their echoes in the dark searched
my flattened stomach for our severed
cord the ghost of its silken thread woven
into cloth that climbs these walls like doubt
and clutters empty corners I can only clean
this house your home in me a hollow place
the cloth a mourning shroud unpicked
the rooms a secret waiting game.

Picking oakum

All day they work, their strong delicate
fingers unpicking the tarred threads
from the tattered ends of old ropes.
Hard work for poor pay, they say
nothing of their gnarled and splintered
fingertips. Even the children don't complain
about the frayed edges and snapped fibres
that shape their waking hours. Tireless,
they gather the heaps of loosened threads
destined for mashing and caulking. They sing
so sweetly, one would almost think they find
pleasure in the rhythm of their work:
in the thankless task of keeping me afloat
as I sit, and stare, and twist more rope.

Loch Ness

Grey ebbs and flows reflect
a sky that has a sun in it
somewhere I saw the signs
blue lines mysterious swells
in dreams I polished every pebble
on this beach I would have been
your mother filled albums with first
uniforms and first bikes and boxes
with small clothes and soft shoes
and myself with the way you would
watch the world
with a slight tilt of the head
one that said *I've seen it all before*
now all I have is this sea-smooth
stone and jagged shore I hurl
into the tidal waters like a trebuchet
wondering who else has thrown
their secrets into this loch only
to have them return
as selkies kelpies
monsters coaxing
their loved ones to drown
in deep and silent grief.

Phonograph

It was real once. The words vibrated in my throat
and filled my body with their music. Now,

the sentiments needled from my heart are faint
and tinny. When I concentrate, my mouth

can echo and amplify the old favourites over
and over. Full of absence, signifying nothing,

all you have is a hollow messenger, a broken record
skipping, faltering, fooling no one because no one is listening.

Except you.
You smile and think every utterance an opus in your honour.

Lighthouse

Before you there was no port
no storm. I lived in open waters
convinced I knew the ground
because I read about it once.

I want the earth. But
there are rocks I did not see
before and rough tides
threaten my small ship.

Your character tells me where
I am, your light how far there is
to go. But I must navigate this sea
and I must find my own way home.

Today is a day for other people's stories

Today I will sit with you   together
we will be the glue   that binds the book
    the space   around the words
the breath   between   the turning pages

Baby blanket

I cast you into the arms of aunts and uncles
and grandparents. They pass you back and forth
like yarn, careful to hide the dropped stitches
and essential tensions holding us together.

Weaving you into our family, they see themselves
in your hair, your ears, your nose. Through you
our tight-knit family repeats itself, generations
of rough shoulders tucked into soft elbows.

Marlfield House

(6th September 2019)

They gather around us like bridesmaids and I
the mother-bride. Precious as a bouquet, they lift
you into their arms, take turns to walk you down

and up the aisle, show you the hydrangeas,
the wedding cake, yourself practising vowels
in the mirror. Slowdanced through dinner

they woo you between courses and tables
with the smiles they save for their children
all sound asleep elsewhere. When it is time

for us to leave, they return you to me, delicate
fragrant sleeping flower, curled into yourself
like a white rose, all easy breaths and unfurled folds.

The bride and groom dance on, love rising and expanding
like bread. I save a slice for later, and we slip away unseen.

The Wanderers

> Oft ic sceolde ana   uhtna gehwylce
> mine ceare cwiþan.

Sharpened by winter's whetstone breath,
we wander like thoughts through this city.
Wrapped up in ourselves we circle hidden
streets: discover shortcuts and laneways
between people and places, times and spaces
that are different now, different then; consider
the labyrinth of cul-de-sacs and local access roads,
ignoring certain avenues with a fixed and forward stare.

And yet, time and time again, we find ourselves
mulling over the same old ground, marvelling
at quiet streets filled with memories pushing past
like Saturday shoppers. Guided by flickering lamps
that hang like family photographs, I push your pram
on narrow paths and imagine walking them alone,
as I must have done. But the streetlights cast you
in every frame, and the memories invite you in for tea
like a long-lost family friend.

The ducks

Out of their depth on land, they waddle
towards us like expectant mothers.
Plump as a Sunday roast from peas
and seeds and porridge oats, they follow
the alms scattered from pond edge
to pram wheels, where you eye them
like an abbot unnerved by their frantic
gratitude. You watch them until the food
is gone and the ground picked clean, until
they drop into the water and swim away
feet floating and falling like sycamore leaves.

Devoted

We slip into our seats and out of our coats
passing you between us like a sign of peace
as the pious chorus sings and souls converge
around our little family. In my arms you
devote yourself to the small black button
on my scarf. They sing to the greatness of God
as your fingers dull and shine its humble surface:
rejoice at being held in His magnificent hands
as you turn it back and forth to catch the light;
and when their voices lift in thanks and exultation,
your mouth holds it like a coin, tests it like a covenant.

On the cusp

Rain tatters on the car roof like fingers
on old phones and hooded students cling

to the kerbs like phantoms. Half-lit by ghostly
screens and full of unfinished business

they carry on their silent conversations
with cold, unseeing eyes. Waiting for a let up

in the traffic, they are indifferent to the rain
needling at them to *get a move on*, noticing

or not noticing how we drive past them
at every junction, condemned to roam

local fields flooded with new streets,
haunted by hard gums and spectral teeth.

Absolution

Cheeks as red as the Passion of Jesus
milk teeth crowd your gums like eager
penitents. With the aches and pangs
of a guilty conscience, they worry
the amber beads of your teething ring
like a decade of the rosary. One by one
they make their confession, pushing
for redemption in the dark humidity
of your innocent mouth. Only then
will they emerge, joyful and triumphant
full of contrition and forgiveness
grace and good intentions.

While the others are away

(after Seamus Heaney)

Him at work, her at school, I sit with you
on the sitting room floor and peel potatoes.
Surrounded by cushions, you watch the knife slice
through each Maris Piper, your hands reaching
grasping, dropping, one by one, the potatoes
halved and heaped between us like playthings,
delighting in the spectacle of the stop and splash,
the satisfied thump and thud of the filling pot.
Job done, you touch your fingers to my lips. I kiss
your hands and they taste of starch, and home.

Squall

In the dead of night I make it rain.
Steam swells and surges into the room
crashing and condensing on frosted
windows and freezing doors. Anchored
beneath the thunderous downpour,
I bail your back with the heel of my hand
as the frantic steam works its way
into the obstructed lining of your lungs
and your tiny chest disgorges the briny
mucus you are drowning in. Only then,
with slow and steadying breaths, can I wash
the ocean from your lips and the tips
of your fingernails. On the bed, a sleeping
turtle plays a tune and its luminous shell
skies the ceiling with coloured stars.

Nita, Sri Lanka, 2005

You pet her coarse mitten hands.
Pinch her stitched toes.
Pat her cotton hair.

'Nita' sewn neatly onto her modest vest.
In Hebrew, it means *Grace*: in Indian, *faithful*.
Native American, *bear*.
(That's what we call you.)

Taller than you,
you look up to her and laugh
at her dark eyes, her curved nose,
her thin red-stitched smile.

She is twelve years old now:
one of twelve thousand made
for the twelve thousand lost.

Your first doll, you will give her
the thoughts and words the tsunami
washed away. You will give her life,
never knowing she has died.

Brough of Birsay, Orkney

I watch the waves break like contractions
against the narrow causeway that joins me

to your father. I count the seconds between
each swell, each desperate centimetre. Head down

shoulders twisted, he muscles through the gusts.
Relentless. I close my eyes, see him as I saw you.

I tell him *It's time*.
Come home. Come home. Come home.

Mother, Nature

Nine million of us watch the shell shatter in high definition
and listen to the yolk drip through sound bars and speakers
with interminable slowness. We *tsk* the cruel nature of the fody bird

and in the same tempered breath wait to comfort ourselves
with the triumph of eggs hatching, or the bumbling majesty
of a fledgling's first flight. Instead, a fairy tern flies into our

living rooms. The once-future mother returning to protect her first
and only egg, she lands with a softness that crushes the breath out of me.
She knows that something isn't quite right Attenborough begins

but her urge to incubate is so strong…

In the pause of nine million swallowed breaths I see the nine-month
journey that brings you to a place where bystanders call for help
and start to mourn but she flies through Special Care until she finds you.

Oblivious of the knowing looks, the readied tears, she nests
into the plastic chair beside you and pours her golden prayers
through the holes in your translucent shell. Feeling only

the urge to incubate, she holds the broken parts of you together
and sits in vigil against the whispers of *permanent damage* and
odds of survival circling your room, auguring your elegy.

Hatchling

Prey to ghost crabs and night birds, footprints
and driftwood, they follow the light of the night-
crested waves, the natural horizon that beckons
and threatens and promises to protect them. Curled
into the shell of my pitted, dimpled stomach we watch
for those who never even fled the nest or for whom
the water's edge became a shallow grave. I watch
for the journey you took to get to me, for the one
in a thousand who makes it to the sea.

Tree frog

Typical of your species, you have long
hind legs and smooth, moist skin. Fingers

and toes spread wide for balance
you unfold yourself at the bottom

of the stairs and stand. Your supple
limbs bear the weight of your swaying

body left to right hand, left to right foot
and up. I follow in your footsteps. All big eyes

and wide mouth, you inspect each step
for inanimate prey: a knot of thread,

a withered leaf, dew drops from a shower
your keen eyes seek to swallow whole.

Our neck of the woods

The flora and fauna of childhood fill every room.
The walls are full of your markings, the house
is full of your scent and still you cannot settle
so we roam the farm tracks and forest trails together
where you transform paths lined with apathetic trees
into living things that whisper *willow* and *ash*, *oak*
and *aspen* as we walk past. The chaffinch asks *do you*
see do you see do you see me here? The blackbird teases
you can't get me you can't get me you can't. There are wildflowers
again and brambles to be stopped at and looked beneath
for berries and badgers hiding from the latent eyes
of passers-by. The tails of lopping rabbits light our
way and we step around potholes waiting for the rain.

Cuckoo

We hit green lights like plate glass windows.
I curse the flow of indifferent traffic
reciting *nappies, wet wipes, bottles, bibs.*

The porch is a nest feathered with school bags
and family photographs. I leave you
and steal away. Childminder chosen

I am free to spend the day
being who I thought I was before.
They tell me this is natural. That I'll get

used to it. But I, I can only walk the hours
until I see you again, gathering twigs, barbed wool,
and scraps of moss, to line my empty pockets.

Maternity leave

The day before
I go back to work
you languish in my arms.
Drifting between versions
of yourself, you toy with a
measuring tape, bemused
by its yellow strip – how far
it can stretch – how quickly
it can all just
(disappear).

Acrania

She saw tall flowers when they said the word
white bluebells in a dawn-strewn wood:
they swayed in ancient silence as she asked them
Is there hope? Two hundred and seventeen

days she has travelled Irish streets. She ignores
the exclamations of old women, acquaintances
accepts the uninvited intimacy of strangers
their questions aired like newlywed linens.
        How long now? Is it a boy or a girl?

It doesn't matter. The coffin will be white.
Knowledge is nothing. By law she carries you.
She will know the sound of your first breath.
The rest is silence.

NOTES

Epidural (30): Inspired by Emily Dickinson's 'After great pain, a formal feeling comes'.

Minute and far away (35): Inspired by F. Scott Fitzgerald's *The Great Gatsby*, the title is a quotation referring to the green light at the end of the Buchanan's dock.

equilibrium (noun) (40): The refrain 'love does not alter' is rooted in Shakespeare's Sonnet 116.

Phonograph (52): The phrase 'signifying nothing' is drawn from Shakespeare's *Macbeth*, Act V Scene 5: 'Life…is a tale told by an idiot, full of sound and fury, signifying nothing.'

Marlfield House (56): The final couplet was inspired by the Pablo Neruda poem beginning 'Crossing the sky I near'.

The Wanderers (57): The epigraph to this poem is from 'The Wanderer', an Anglo-Saxon poem found in *The Exeter Book*. Translated by S.A.J. Bradley in *Anglo-Saxon Poetry* (Everyman, 1982) it reads 'Often I have had to bemoan my anxieties alone at each dawning.'

While the others are away (62): Inspired by Seamus Heaney's poem 'When all the others were away at Mass' from 'Clearances'.

Nita, Sri Lanka, 2005 (64): After the devastating tsunami that struck Sri Lanka in December 2004, an initiative was started in Cork, Ireland, to make 12,000 Nino dolls which were sold to aid the relief effort.

Mother, Nature (66): The quotation from David Attenborough is taken from *Planet Earth II*: Episode 1, 'Islands'.

Acrania (73): The final line comes from Shakespeare's *Hamlet*, Act V Scene 2.

ACKNOWLEDGEMENTS

Acknowledgements are due to the editors of the following publications in which some of these poems, or versions of them, have previously appeared: *Banshee Lit, Butcher's Dog, Coast to Coast to Coast, Finished Creatures, Gutter, The Interpreter's House, The Irish Times, Magma, New Writing Scotland, Northwords Now, Poetry Ireland Review, RAUM, Stand, The Stinging Fly*, and *Under the Radar*.

'Acrania' and 'Hermit Crab' were shortlisted for the Hennessy New Irish Writing Award 2018. 'The Wanderers' was made into a filmpoem, directed and produced by Ted Fisher, in collaboration with Magma and the University of Edinburgh (2018). Thanks, Ted, for the beautiful cover image. 'Sounds of that day' appeared in *New Scottish Writing* #38 and *Staying Human: new poems for Staying Alive* (Bloodaxe Books, 2020); 'Ubi Sunt' also appeared in *Staying Human*.

An immeasurable debt of thanks is due to those who have helped shape this collection through careful reading and thoughtful advice: Leeanne Quinn, Heather Parry, Helen Sedgwick, Niall Campbell, Mr (Kevin) Honan and, of course, Neil Astley. Thanks are also due to Hollie McNish for her support for this book.

For the friends and family who have loved me through everything: Nathalie Ennis, Meghanne Flynn, Karina Jakubowicz, Louise Kemény, Shona MacKenzie, Georgina Nugent-Folan and Orla Sweeney. You have done more for me than you will ever know.

For my husband, Simon, my best friend now and always.

And finally, for my mother, Patricia Griffin, a force of nature in her own right.